Focus

The focus of this book is:

- to develop the children's speaking and listening skills through mind mapping,
- to use a contents page to find specific information.

Tuning In

The front cover

Let's read the title together.

If you were going to answer that question (How does water change?), what would you say?

The back cover

Let's read the blurb and see if the book is going to answer the question in the same way we did.

Is this what we expected the book to be about?

Contents

How many different forms can water have?

Let's read the list of contents together.

We are going to choose which section to read-Liquids, Solids or Gases, but first we are going to read the introdution.

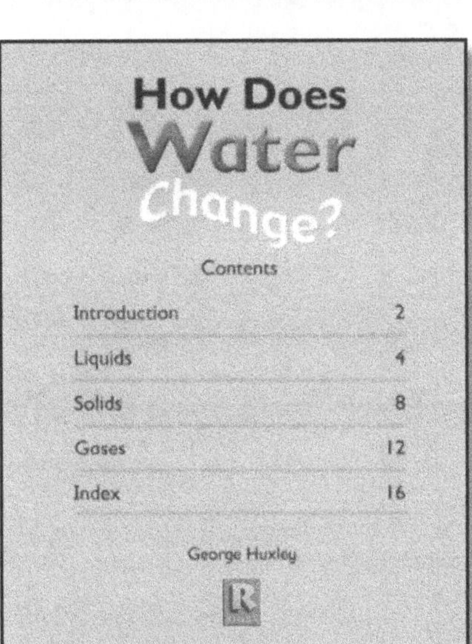

 ## Tuning In

What are the different forms of water we can have?

 ## Observe and Prompt

Word Recognition

- Check the children are using their decoding skills to tackle the words on these pages, such as 'Water', 'forms' and 'solid'.

- If the children have difficulty reading 'liquid', model the blending of this word for them.

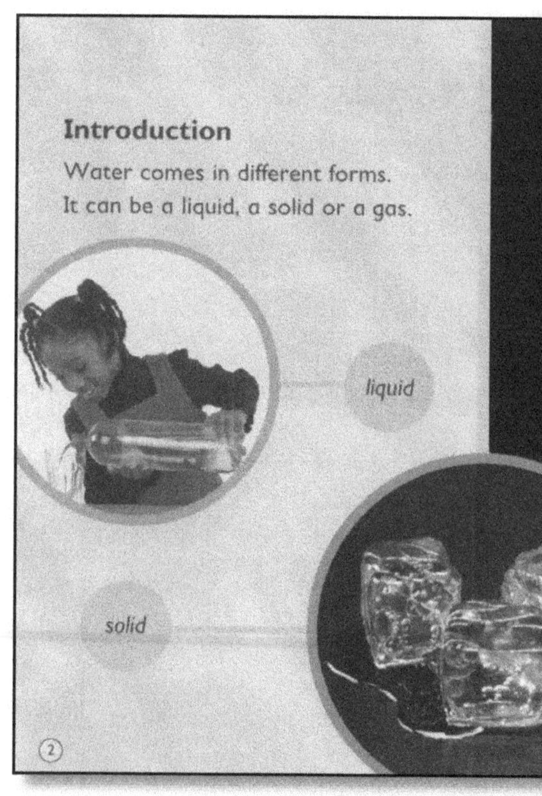

Observe and Prompt

Language Comprehension

- Ask the children what the words in circles show.

- Ask the children if they know what water is called when it is a gas. *(steam)*

- Ask the children to go back to the contents and choose a section to read.

 **Tuning In**

Why is the girl able to pour the water easily?

 **Observe and Prompt**

Word Recognition

- Check the children can read the sight words confidently on this page, such as 'is', 'the' and 'you'.

Liquids

When water is in a liquid form, it moves freely. The water in the glass is in a liquid form.

Where else can you find water in a liquid form?

Observe and Prompt

Language Comprehension

- Check that the children are noticing the punctuation as they read.

- Ask the children to read the question in italics again. *Where else do we find liquid water?*

 **Tuning In**

How does the water in a river move?

 **Observe and Prompt**

Word Recognition

- Help the children with the vowel sound in 'moves' if they have difficulty with this word.

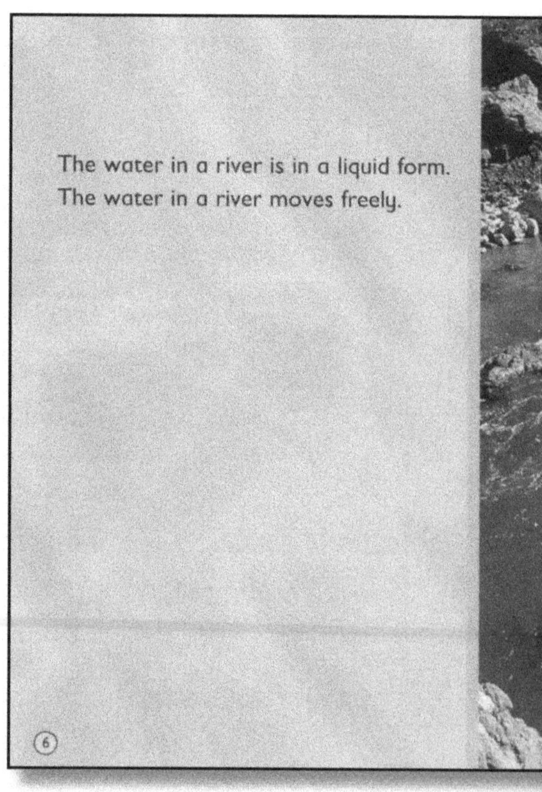

 **Observe and Prompt**

> ## Language Comprehension
>
> - Ask the children how the water moves in a river.
> - Have any of the children in the class ever seen a river like this?

 **Tuning In**

How does water feel when it is solid?

How is water different when it is a solid?

What is the photograph of?

 **Observe and Prompt**

Word Recognition

- Help the children with the 'a' sound in 'shape' (from 'a' and silent 'e'), if they have difficulty with this word.

Solids

When water is in a solid form, it is hard. It keeps its shape.

Where else can you find water in a solid form?

8

 **Observe and Prompt**

Language Comprehension

- Ask the children what solid water is called. *(ice)*

- Ask the children where else they can find water as a solid.

Tuning In

What is the photograph of?

Is an iceberg made of water?

 ## Observe and Prompt

Word Recognition

- If the children have difficulty reading 'iceberg', prompt them to split the word down into two syllables, before blending the whole word together.

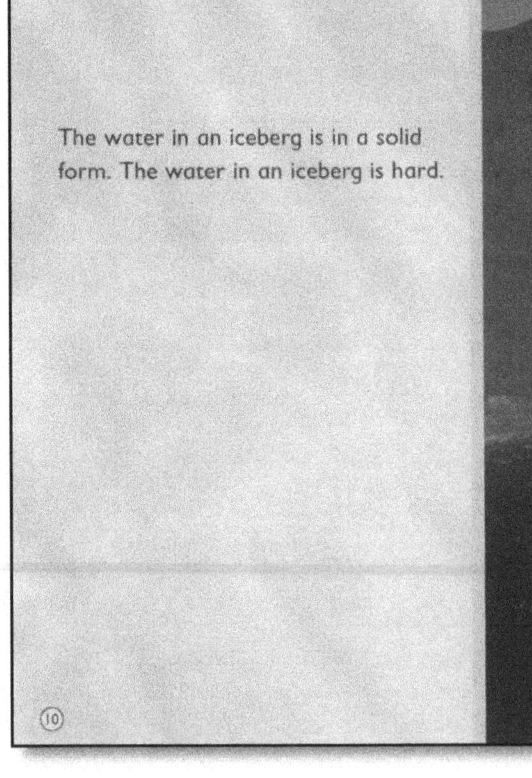

The water in an iceberg is in a solid form. The water in an iceberg is hard.

(10)

 **Observe and Prompt**

Language Comprehension

- Check the children understand what an iceberg is.

- Where do the children think icebergs can be found?

 **Tuning In**

Look at the steam coming out of the kettle.
What has happened to the water inside
the kettle?

 **Observe and Prompt**

Word Recognition

- Check that the children understand that the phoneme /e/ can be spelt 'ea', as in 'spreads' and 'e', as in 'kettle'.

- Help the children with the 'ea' sound in 'steam' if they struggle with this word.

- Model the reading of 'air' if necessary.

Gases

When water is in the form of a gas, it spreads through the air.

The steam that rises from a kettle of boiling water is in the form of a gas.

Where else can you find water in the form of a gas?

(12)

 **Observe and Prompt**

Language Comprehension

- Ask the children what we call water when it is a gas.

- Why do the children think they should never put their hand near steam?

 **Tuning In**

In some places in the world, lakes and pools are very hot from the earth underneath. We call these 'hot springs'.

What can you see in the photograph?

 **Observe and Prompt**

Word Recognition

- Help the children with the long 'i' sound in 'rises' (from 'i' and silent 'e') if they struggle with this word.

- If the children have difficulty reading 'through', model the blending of this word for them.

14

 **Observe and Prompt**

Language Comprehension

- Ask the children where the steam is rising from here.

- Ask the children what happens to the steam as it rises.

 **Tuning In**

This page is called an index. What would we use it for?

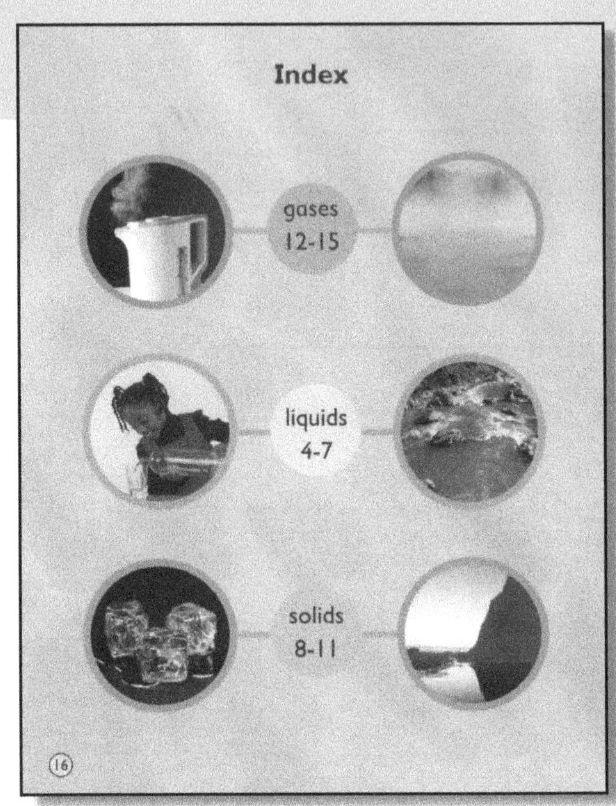

 **Observe and Prompt**

Language Comprehension

- Check the children understand the purpose of an index and can use it effectively.

- Ask the children to use the index to look up information about 'liquids'.